Deer

Deer

Mary Berendes

THE CHILD'S WORLD®, INC.

Library of Congress Cataloging-in-Publication Data
Berendes, Mary.
Deer / by Mary Berendes.
p.   cm.
Includes index.
Summary: Describes the physical characteristics,
behavior, habitat, and life cycle of deer.
ISBN 1-56766-586-1 (lib. bdg. : alk paper)
1. Deer—Juvenile literature.
[1. Deer.]   I. Title.
QL737.U55B46   1999
599.65—dc21   98-33999
CIP
AC

Photo Credits

© Beth Davidow/WorldWild: 20
© Byron Jorjorian/Tony Stone Images: 9
© 1993 Craig Brandt: 10
© Daniel J. Cox/Natural Exposures, Inc.: 13, 23, 26
© Gene Boaz: 29
© 1994 George E. Stewart/Dembinsky Photo Assoc. Inc.: 24
© 1998 Michael H. Francis: 6
© Patrick Grace, The National Audubon Society Collection/Photo Researchers: 15
© Rich Kirchner: 19
© 1993 Skip Moody/Dembinsky Photo Assoc. Inc.: 16
© 1994 Skip Moody/Dembinsky Photo Assoc. Inc.: 2
© Stephen J. Krasemann, The National Audubon Society Collection/Photo Researchers: 30
© Tom and Pat Leeson: cover

On the cover...

Front cover: This *white-tailed deer* is listening for danger.
Page 2: This white-tailed deer is standing in some flowers.

Table of Contents

Early on a fall morning, the meadow is quiet. A cool breeze blows slowly through the tall grass. At the far edge of the meadow, you see a creature. It walks slowly, turning its head and listening for danger. Suddenly, the animal hears a noise and bounds away. What was this beautiful animal? It was a deer!

⇐ This white-tailed deer is taking a morning walk in a Texas meadow.

What Do Deer Look Like?

Deer belong to a group of animals called **mammals.** Mammals have hair on their bodies and have warm blood. They also feed their babies milk from their bodies. Dogs and people are mammals, too.

Deer are beautiful animals. They have large eyes on the sides of their heads. They have shiny hair and short tails. They also have long ears and skinny legs.

This white-tailed deer lives near the Great Smoky Mountains. ⇒

Are There Different Kinds of Deer?

There are more than 60 kinds, or **species,** of deer. They have names such as *elk, moose, red deer, mule deer,* and *reindeer.* Some deer grow to be very large. The moose is the largest deer in the world. It can grow to be over seven feet tall and weigh almost 2,000 pounds!

The *pudu* is the smallest deer. It lives in the warm forests of South America. It only stands about one foot tall and weighs about 15 pounds.

The most common deer in North America is the *white-tailed deer.* This deer is named for the fluffy white underside of its tail. When a white-tailed deer is frightened, it runs and leaps away from danger. As it runs, it lifts its tail to show the white part. This lets other deer know that danger is nearby.

This male whitetail is listening for danger in a Wisconsin forest. ⇒

How Do Deer Run?

A deer's foot is really two toes. Each of the toes is protected by a hard covering called a **hoof.** The hooves help the deer push off from the ground as it runs. By running on its "tiptoes," a deer can run 40 miles per hour and leap 20 feet! The hooves can also be used to fight off enemies. A deer's hooves can be very sharp— one strong kick can really hurt an attacker.

It is easy to see the two toes of this moose's foot. ⇒

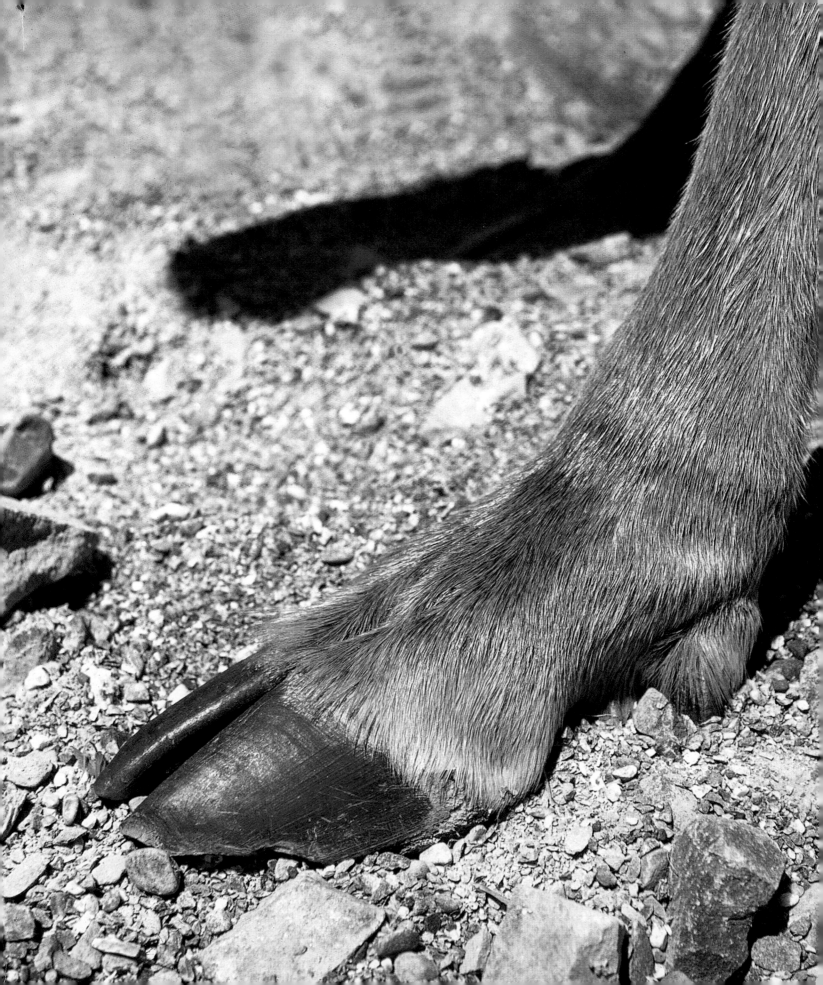

Deer are the only animals with **antlers.** Antlers are very hard bones that grow out of a deer's head. Most male deer have antlers. Some female deer, such as reindeer, also have antlers.

Antlers come in many shapes. Some deer's antlers are round and flat. Others are thin and pointed. Deer use their antlers to protect themselves from enemies. They also use them for fighting with other deer.

⇐ This male whitetail has beautiful antlers.

Once a year, a deer's antlers fall off. After a short time, new ones begin to grow. A deer's new antlers are soft and tender. They are covered with a thin layer of skin called **velvet.** The velvet is very soft and fuzzy. When the antlers are done growing, the velvet dries up. Then the deer scrapes it off on trees and bushes.

A deer's antlers grow back bigger each year. At first, a deer's antlers are short and straight. But as the deer grows older, its antlers get longer. They even form branches!

This male *caribou* is losing its velvet. ⇒

Some deer live in hot, dry deserts. Others live in colder, northern areas. Most deer, though, like to make their homes on prairies, in swamps, or in green forests that have mild weather.

Unlike other animals, deer do not make homes, dens, or nests. Instead, they spend their lives roaming in a large area called a **home range.** Within their home range, deer search for food and raise their babies.

⇐ This *elk* has a huge home range in Yellowstone National Park.

What Are Male and Female Deer Called?

Male and female deer have different names, depending on their species. Most male deer are called **bucks.** But moose, elk, and reindeer males are called *bulls*. Male red deer are called *stags*.

Most female deer are called **does.** But moose, elk, and reindeer females are called *cows*. Red deer females are called *hinds*.

This *mule deer* doe is searching for food in a snowy Montana forest. ⇒

Six to 10 months after a male and female deer mate, a baby deer is born. Most baby deer are called **fawns.** Caribou, elk, moose, and reindeer babies are called *calves.* At first, a baby deer wobbles and falls when it tries to stand up. Soon, though, it is running and jumping alongside its mother.

Baby deer stay very close to their mother. They learn how to eat and how to stay safe just by watching her. When the young deer are old enough, they leave their mother and go off to find their own places to live.

← This whitetail fawn is watching its mother as she eats nearby.

All deer are plant-eaters, or **herbivores.** In the warm spring months, they eat grasses, flowers, and budding leaves. When these plants dry up in the hot summer weather, deer find twigs, stems, and green leaves to munch on.

During the winter, it is harder for deer to find food. They must dig and stamp in the snow with their hooves to uncover frozen plants and twigs. If they are really hungry, deer will also eat tree bark or branches.

⇐ This female elk is eating grass on a flooded Wyoming meadow.   27

Do Deer Have Any Enemies?

Deer have many enemies. Bears, wolves, and coyotes all like to hunt deer for food. Many people like to hunt deer, too. To stay safe, deer are very careful animals. They are always listening, smelling, and watching for any signs of danger. When they sense that an enemy is near, they quickly leave the area by running, leaping, or walking.

This white-tailed deer is listening for danger as she walks along. ⇒

Not very long ago, deer had plenty of space in which to live and eat. Today, however, many deer must share their spaces with people. To keep deer safe, many cities and towns have set aside nature areas. No buildings or machines are allowed in these areas, so the deer can live safely and happily. By cooperating with deer and sharing the land, we can make sure there will always be wonderful deer for people to see.

Glossary

antlers (ANT–lerz)
Antlers are bones that grow out of a deer's head. There are many different sizes and shapes of antlers.

bucks (BUKS)
Most male deer are called bucks.

does (DOHZ)
Most female deer are called does.

fawns (FAWNZ)
Most baby deer are called fawns.

herbivores (HER–bih-vorz)
Herbivores are animals that eat only plants. Deer are herbivores.

home range (HOME RAINJ)
A home range is the area a deer lives in. Some home ranges are very large.

hoof (HOOF)
A hoof is the hard covering on a deer's foot.

mammals (MA–mullz)
Mammals are animals that have hair, warm blood, and feed their babies milk from their bodies. Dogs and people are mammals, too.

species (SPEE–sheez)
A species is a different kind of an animal. There are over 60 species of deer.

velvet (VELL–vet)
Velvet is the soft, fuzzy skin that covers a deer's new antlers. When the velvet dries up, the deer rubs it off on trees and bushes.

Index